CHARACTERWORKS – The Actors Process
by Acting Coach John Pallotta
ISBN: 9798507481101

CW00502178

CHARACTERWORKS
The *Art* of Emotional Triggering

-CREATING THE CHARACTER-

JOHN PALLOTTA

CHARACTERWORKS

THE ACTORS PROCESS
CREATING THE CHARACTER
Acting Coach John Pallotta
VOL. IV

*As an acting coach I have
an innate, absolute love for seeing my actors
blossom into something that might even surprise them.*

John Pallotta

KIND WORDS

*If John Pallotta were a boxer,
he'd be Jake LaMotta.
A singer? Johnny Cash.
Coffee? Triple espresso.
An award? Most definitely The Oscar.*

*James Brown
3X Emmy Winner*

*Always listen to what John Pallotta
Has to say.
He's got a good heart,
His head is in the right place.
He'll set you straight*

*Kevin Kline
Oscar, Emmy, Tony Winner*

ISBN: 9798507481101

OUR LIVES AS ACTORS

"Our lives as actors are filled with actors who enter from stage left and exit stage right. Some people show up in every scene, some only a few, providing punctuation to the real action. We wait for the invisible hand that's writing the story of our life that needs a sweet small voice to explain the themes for our audience.

We strike a balance, life becomes an art form, each choice we make on is precious, and every chance for creativity is an opportunity. And yet we struggle with the meaning of it all, to varying degrees. We would like to believe that the truly blessed people don't bother with the struggle and just have fun."

John Pallotta

Other Books by
Acting Coach John Pallotta can be found at
www.actorstheater.com

NOTE TO THE READER

Almost every acting class in the world trains actors to "play an objective", in other words, to choose an action based on the information you get from reading the script, or, why the character is doing what he is doing. Believe me, that's the easy part of dealing with actions. The piece of the puzzle that few actors learn to deal with is the deeper, personal layer of "why" they are playing those actions.

Please consider this acting fact. Without a personal need to accomplish the "action", you have not yet earned your right to stand on that stage and speak the words of the script. I am talking about having the true need to do the things you are doing in the play. The "true need". Not the pretended need or the indicated need, but the authentic need. Having the true need to do what you are doing, is the seed of all life on stage.

Isn't this true in life? Yes, in life, your actions are purposeful, you have the true need to do the things you do in each moment or you would not bother doing them. It is the same on the stage - we call this "purpose", your acting must be truly purposeful.

Remember, theatre is not an imitation of our lives, it demands a greater truth. "True purpose" is an essential part of that greater truth."

ACTING COACH JOHN PALLOTTA

John Pallotta is a master on-camera acting teacher and one of the most sought-after acting coaches in the industry today. John has almost 40 years of experience as an actor, playwright, director, producer and acting coach and has trained under such masters as Lee Strasberg (Institute), Stella Adler, Bobbie Lewis, Uta Hagen, Austin Pendleton, Wynn Handman as well as many others. John Pallotta's belief is that "Acting is A State of Mind". Today, that belief has become an industry standard in John's books and in his teachings across the country.

John has accomplished thousands of coaching sessions and has ignited and reignited the careers of some of the talent you see on TV today: including Emmy award winner Anna Maria Chlumsky, Emmy Winner Johnny Alonso and many more.

John Pallotta has written 23 plays for the stage and his works have been produced, read, developed and workshopped at such venues as the Actors studio in New York City, Steppenwolf Theatre in Chicago, The Labyrinth Theatre in NYC Playwrights Horizons in NYC as well as may venues across the United States.

John's focus as a teacher of the craft is to help each and every one of his students find their own voice as an actor. Acting is a process. It is a journey of discovery. It is a living breathing process that happens each and every day and does not happen overnight. Becoming an actor is learning a new way of thinking and about the way you look at life. Just as you make choices in life that determine your success or your failure. It goes the same for your choices you make as an actor.

GIVING THANKS

For actors giving thanks can feel like an art form all in itself. As an actor, it can be easy to get swept away when your job is all about you. Entitlement, ego, or the promise of material things can make it harder to appreciate what we already have. These traps can even cause us to forget why we love what we do in the first place. That's why giving thanks is so important. For some of us, we were trained to serve an art and not be self-serving.

Thank your mentors and professional colleagues at every opportunity. I believe it is necessary to express gratitude to those who have nurtured us, extended professional courtesies and opportunities to us, and inspired us. But most of all, helped us develop as actors, artists and human beings

WHAT ACTORS SHOULD BE THANKFUL FOR

Other actors - to share and collaborate with
The crew - for pulling the productions together
The creatives - for putting in the effort to develop every production
The audience - for appreciating the productions
The representation - for working on your behalf
The experience - of acting, creating, and learning
The paycheck - for showing your work is appreciated in that way
The freedom - to express and pursue what you want
The relationships - you develop along the way
The expression - that comes with acting your heart out
The privilege - of pursuing your passions
The process - of preparing & the journey with no destination
The challenge - that forces you to work hard to better yourself
The discovery - of yourself and your characters in your work

So even though things may not always go your way, take a moment every now and then to think about the things that make your life as an actor something so very special.

TABLE OF CONTENTS

Introduction	2-7
Screen Acting Tips for Film and Television	8
Analyzing your Character	13
Characters Given Circumstances	15
Character Development	17
Creating the Character Through Costumes	21
Telling the Story Through Props	22
Actors Understanding Camera Angles	23
Self-Taping for Actors – The New Norm	25
Be on your "A" Game with Audition Drills	29
The Branded Actor	32
Social Media in the Actors World	36
Audition Drills level I	42
Audition Drills Level II	46
CLOSING	102

BASIC SCREEN ACTING TIPS FOR FILM AND TELEVISION

Acting for film and television is a skill set separate from the theatre. In addition to all of the challenges faced when acting in a theatrical context, Screen Acting has its own unique set of technical, logistical, and creative obstacles (and opportunities), and is a skill set honed over time through training and experience in front of the camera. The great screen actors have these techniques mastered.

YOUR EYES ARE THE WINDOW INTO YOUR SOUL

The camera captures every moment; what you're thinking, what you're feeling, your internal conflicts, and your physical impulses. What's more, it can get all of this through your eyes. Treat them like magnets. They pull the viewer into the soul of the person you're portraying. Imagine a rectangle around the lens, and when in thoughts or transitions between lines, allow the lens to see what you're thinking and feeling by giving the camera your eyes. The closer the frame, the tighter the rectangle for you.

TREAT THE SILENCES AS LINES AND BE THE EDITOR'S FRIEND

No moment should be missed, no emotional stone unturned. Emotional investment in only your lines are not enough. Every moment and beat needs to be considered. What is the other character saying to you, and how is it affecting you? **Film and television editing requires reaction shots;** they are integral to the flow of the narrative and character development. The editor will be looking for those reactions in post production. By treating the pauses and silences in the script as lines themselves, imbued with intention and thought, you will find a greater depth to your performance and connection with the other character(s) in the scene. You'll probably bag more screen time because of it!

KNOW YOUR AUDIENCE

Unlike the theatre, there is no live audience. There is a lengthy and important post production process that happens between your performance and the viewing public. Your audience is not present when you film, and this needs to be remembered when you are on set. The director isn't the audience, the crew aren't the audience, the camera operator isn't the audience, the camera isn't your audience, the only audience you have are within the fictional realms of the narrative, and the other characters that inhabit it. Resist, at all costs, to perform for the crew.

BE PREPARED AND FLEXIBLE

You will film out of sequence on set. Schedules change all the time. Not only do you have to be prepared in terms of your character journey at every moment in the story, but also for last minute changes to the plan of the filming process. There are so many varying factors; weather, daylight hours, transportation issues, technical glitches, that you do not want to be one of them. Be prepared to step on set and only get two or three takes to get it right. Don't let your first take be a rehearsal or a warm up. Full character preparation will assist you in getting in getting it right first time. It will also help you to change your performance in the ways that the director wants in the next takes. By fluid and flexible, and in doing so you won't only give a more nuanced performance, but you'll also have a much better working relationship with the director and the crew.

LEARN THE JARGON AND WHO'S ON SET

Be versed in the technical language of the film set. Know which person does which job on set, the jargon that they use, and how they operate. Know the shot sizes and the intended camera movement from onset discussions, so you don't have to ask the DOP or director all the time. Film and television require many different departments working simultaneously to produce a final product. You are a piece of that jigsaw puzzle, no more or less important than all the rest of the pieces. By knowing your way round a film set you are instantly respectful of everyone's important job within the process, and as a result you will be painless to work with. Don't underestimate **the power of being polite and easy to work with**, repeat work will come your way because of the positive way you conduct yourself.

I. Basic Screen Acting Etiquette:

1. Always keep going until the director shouts "Cut!" and then keep on acting for a bit.
2. If you mess up a line, keep going until the director call a halt to the take. Let it be HIS decision.
3. Do not stop a take for **any** reason, except for possible injury or death.
4. Never look directly into the camera lens unless specifically requested to do so.
5. Never ask the director what size of shot it is – ask the camera operator.
6. Hit your mark! Being in the right place is often more important than saying the right line.
7. Maintain your concentration and eyelines all through the tedium of lineup and rehearsal; it helps both your fellow actors **and** the crew.
8. An actor only has status between "Action!" and "Cut!" Exception: A star may have it all the time.
9. Never say you do not want to play a role; say that you are unavailable. Never say "No," say "Maybe" instead.

II. The Camera Lens:

1. Generally, ignore the camera lens; let it "find and reveal" you.
2. Don't merely cheat an eyeline, motivate it.
3. If both your eyes cannot "see" the camera lens, your face will appear to be obscured.
4. Keep on an imaginary narrow path that stretches out from the front of the camera. Remember that shots are composed in depth, not width.
5. In a 3-shot, put the lens in the middle of the gap, not yourself.
6. If you have trouble hitting a mark, line up 2 objects at the final position you have to hit. Establish a "web."

7. Shoulders angled toward the camera often look better than straight-on ones.

III. The Frame:

1. When doing commercials, cheat all business, hands (gestures), and important props (product) up into the "hot" area in closeups.
2. Adjust your acting style within the frame according to the size of shot:
a. Long Shot = large gestures/scale – back of the house (theatre)
b. Medium Shot = smaller scale, intimate arena theatre, theatrical reality.
c. Medium Close Up = Actual reality; the real thing
d. Extreme Close Up = Very intimate; think it, put all concentration/energy into your face.
3. Be prepared to stand embarrassing close when acting and speaking with other characters.
4. There is no reality outside the frame; time and/or distance outside the frame may be expanded or contracted.

IV. Vocal Tips:

1. Project only as far as your fellow actor(s).
2. Intensity can be created by increasing enunciation and pace, not volume.
3. When the camera is moving with you (tracking), talk fast but move slow.
4. If you are told to tone it all down, try reducing only your volume but keeping the scale of your gestures (such notes usually refer to the voice).
5. Be aware that when speaking with a strong accent there is a tendency to speak louder – don't.
6. With a studio audience, if they can hear you without the benefit of microphones, you are probably speaking too loudly.
7. Never project louder than the star (or regulars on a series). They set the style for the program.
8. When speaking at low levels, all other sounds seem too loud, so take care with all footsteps, clattering cups, newspaper rustling – even breathing.
9. When speaking at low levels, do not lose energy or adopt a slower pace.
10. As the scene builds, you would expect the voices to rise, but since the shots are liable to get tighter, you have to square the circle by getting more intense – and quieter – at the same time.
11. Gently ask if you are going to be in a contained 2-shot, or if they are going to cross-cut with reverses, in which case be prepared to not overlap dialogue.

V. Acting for the Camera:

1. Your main acting note is the you were given the part, so work your looks, personality, and background into your performance. Use yourself. That is what they purchased.
2. The shots the director chooses are in themselves acting notes, so obey their implicit instructions: a. Long Shot = allow your body to do the talking. b. Reaction shot = do a reaction (even if you feel you are "pulling faces").
c. Two-shot + react as you listen to the other actor.
d. Close-up = put your thoughts onto your face.
e. Close-up of your hand holding a prop = channel your acting and thoughts into that.

3. Do all your acting to an Audience of One – the other player (the camera will pick you up).

4. Create good acting reasons for all your pieces of business (including camera-motivating ones).

5. Learn your lines well. They should fit you like a glove. If they don't, and you don't have the rehearsal time to create the character who would say those lines, then ask to change them.

6. Find positive ways of communicating negative thoughts.

7. Give yourself something to do after a shot ends!!! This will keep your face alive right to the end of the take.

8. Let your inner voice give you those continuous instructions that silent movie actors got from their directors' megaphones.

9. Let an acting impulse that would lead to a move on stage lead to a gesture or look on the screen.

10. When the camera is on you in a single shot, it is as if you were alone on a stage and the other performers were in the wings: now how do you act?

VI. The Editor:

1. The better your continuity, the easier it is for the editor to cut to you for your best moments.

2. Editors like to cut on movements, so put some in before one of your important bits of acting.

3. Mark changes of thought with appropriate pieces of business.

4. During a speech, look at the other characters. The editor needs your "eyeflashes" to motivate cuts.

5. Reactions don't have to be logical or consistent. The editor is only looking for a slice of a good reaction, and several different ones give him/her a better choice (to cut to you!).

VII. Reactions and Business:

1. React before you speak and react to the upcoming thought. This is best done on the intake of breath before the line.

2. React while others are speaking – on screen we watch the listening character.

3. The best moments are nonverbal ones – so give yourself time.

4. Learn all your lines and business in advance of the shoot very very well. During the shoot you will be concentrating on all the new things, such as remembering camera angles and hitting marks. But also, be prepared to change lines and business at the very last moment – be flexible in a very cooperative way.

5. Pace consists of continuous events, not continuous speaking.

6. Fully motivate any large reactions. Don't reduce your size, increase your believability.

7. Remember the camera cannot follow fast movements, so lift that cup slowly, gently rise up out of that chair.

8. In a multicamera studio a red light means the camera is on, so keep a reaction on your face until it has been sampled by that camera.

9. Eyes can be very effective. Try looking up as well as down, especially when "listening" to another character. Some try looking from one eye to the other.

10. At an interview and reading, plan at least one major reaction in the middle of a reading. Remember to react during the "feed" lines, and to keep your eyes up.

VIII. Some Final Thoughts:

1. To come across as truthful and believable needs both talent, technique, and brains.

2. Don't panic over any problem. There has never been a trouble-free shoot, and anyway tomorrow's problem is already in the mail.

3. Don't do today's job as an audition for tomorrow. Do it because this is what you want to do today. Play for the moment at hand. Concentrate on

4. All rules are made to be broken – so know which rules you are breaking! And have a good reason for doing so.

5. If screen acting is going to be a very important part of your career, find out how to enjoy and relish it all. If you allow it, it can (and should) be a lot of fun.

ANALYZING YOUR CHARACTER

THE ACTOR MUST KNOW THE ANSWER TO EVERY QUESTION, THOUGH THE CHARACTER.

PHYSICAL QUALITIES

Who am I?
Who am I named after? Do I like my name?
What is my gender? What do I think about sex?
How old am I?
How does my posture express my age, health, inner feeling?
How is my complexion? What do I think of it?
What is my height? What do I think of I?
What is my weight? What do I think of it?
What is the pitch, volume, tempo, resonance or quality of my voice? What do I think of it?
Do I have a dialect or accent?
What is my hair color and style? Do I like it?
Do I have any deformities? What do I think of them?
Do I have any mannerisms? What do I think of them?
Do I have any handicaps? What do I think of them?
How energetic or vital am I? Do I like it?
Do I suffer from any disease's past or present?
Do I like my walk?
How do I usually sit?
How do I usually stand?
Do I have any objects, hand props or accessories with me? Why? How do I handle them?
What do I like to wear? What do I have to wear? How do I wear my clothes? How do I handle them?

SOCIAL QUALITIES

What do I do when I wake up each morning?
What is my relationship to my environment? Do I like it?
What is my educational background? How much discipline was I subjected to? How intelligent am I?
What was my childhood like? What are my strongest memories?
How much money do I have? How much do I want?
What is my nationality? What do I think of it?
What is my occupation? Do I like it? What other jobs have I had? When and why did I choose this one?
What are my political attitudes?
Am I religious?
What are my religious beliefs?
Did I have childhood heroes? What did I like about them?

Do I like members of the opposite sex? What do I like about them?
Who were my parents? What do I like and/or dislike about them?
Do I like my family? What do I like? What do I dislike?
How has my mother influenced me? How has my father influenced me?
Do I have brothers and sisters? What do I think about them?
What was my favorite fairy tale? Why?
Who are my friends? Who are my enemies? How can I tell if someone is a friend or an enemy?
What ideas do I like? What ideas do I dislike?
What hobbies or interests do I have?
Do I have children? Do I like them? Why? Do they like me?
What advice do I have for my children?
Am I married? Why did I marry the person I did?
What do I think about my spouse? What do I dislike?
How do my physical traits affect each of the social traits?
How do the social traits affect the script and my objective?
How do the social traits affect my life needs and wants?

PSYCHOLOGICAL QUALITIES

What choices do I face?
What choices do I make?
What makes me angry? What relaxes me?
What are my driving ambitions, my goals?
Do I do things impulsively?
What do I worry about?
What do I want? What do others think I want?
What do I like about myself? Dislike about myself?
What do I need?
What do I fear?
Why can't I get what I want?
Do other people like me? Why?
Are any of my psychological traits manifested physically?
Are any of my psychological traits manifested vocally?

MORAL QUALITIES

Are the choices I will make based upon expediency of some ethical standard?
Who do I admire?
Will the pursuit of my needs lead to a moral choice?
What is my attitude toward the choice I make?
How do I express this attitude vocally and physically?
Does your decision ring any bells in your head saying this is a bad choice?
Does your decision(s) question the authority of any laws, policies, or procedures?
Does your decision withstand the light of day?
How does your decisions in the scene effect the people around you?

Would a person you look up to make this same decision, or would they be disappointed in your choice of action?
Would you want someone to do this to you?

THE GIVEN CIRCUMSTANCES

The given circumstances are the aspects of the world of the scene that the script tells us. Sometimes the scene tells us the given circumstances directly, other times the actors need to figure it out through close reading. The given circumstances should be clear to the audience to help them understand the context of what they are watching. After reading the script, answer the questions below.

Title of Scene: _____

Name of character: _____

Time

What were you doing 10 minutes before the scene started?

_____

What were you doing 24hours before the scene started?

_____

What is the time of day for each scene?

_____

What is the time of year for each scene?

_____

Period

What is the year, or general time period? _

_____

Place

Where does the action take place? Describe it. • Is the place inside or outdoors?

_____

What furniture pieces are needed?

_____

Are there any doors or windows needed?

Locale

What is the general location of where the scene takes place?

Theme

What ideas does the scene make you think about?

What does your character want above all else?

Are there any actions, words, or ideas that appear throughout the script?

What lesson does the audience learn by the end of the scene?

Mood

How does the character make you feel? Brainstorm feeling/words.

DEVELOPMENT OF YOUR CHARACTER

One of your jobs as an actor is to flesh out and create a total life for your character. You must become completely comfortable inhabiting the language and actions of your character. To aid and assist you in this task complete the following questions as your character would. Your answers must be based on facts and clues given by the writer (given circumstances).

There are no right or wrong answers except for specific information given by the writer. Questions not answered with information provided by the playwright can be based on your own intuition, creativity and imagination. On a separate sheet of paper answer the questions as completely and in as much detail as possible.

All these tools developed by Acting Coach John Pallotta are only really useful if you use them right. Here are a few suggestions to help you get the most out of your character.

Start by browsing quickly over all of the questions to get a sense of the sections

Vary how you use the questionnaire depending on the character / the day / your mood

Pick out the questions that you find work best for you, and use them to create your own personal streamlined questionnaire

Completely ignore any sections you don't feel are relevant to your character

Mix it up - one day you might decide to pick 10 questions completely at random. Another day you might decide to complete all the questions in a single section.

Approach it as a brainstorming exercise

Allow your mind to go down a rabbit hole, if one question inspires you to write an entire scene from that character's history, then fantastic!

Understand that your in-depth knowledge of the character will bleed into your writing, even if the vast majority of this information is never written in your manuscript.

100 QUESTIONS YOU ASK FROM YOUR CHARACTERS POINT OF VIEW

LEVEL ONE

1. What is your full name?
2. What else are you called? (nickname?)

3. What is your sex?

4. What is your age?

5. What is your height and weight?

6. What color are your hair, eyes, skin, etc.?

7. What sort of posture do you have?

8. What is your overall appearance? (good-looking, over- or underweight, clean, neat, pleasant, untidy. Shape of head, face, limbs, etc.

9. Any defects? (deformities, abnormalities, birthmarks, diseases)

10. What about your ancestors and heredity?

11. Where do you live? (city, state, country)

12. Where were you born?

13. When is your birthday? (day, month, year)

14. What class of society are you? (working, ruling, middle, petite bourgeoisic)

15. What is your occupation? (type of work, hours of work, income, condition of work, work ethic, union or non-union, attitude toward organization, suitability for your work)

16. What is your education? (amount, kind of schools, marks, favorite subjects, poorest subjects, aptitudes.)

17. What about your home life? (parents living, earning power, orphan, parents separated or divorced, parents' habits, parents' mental development, parents' vices, neglect)

18. What is your marital status?

19. Do you have any brothers and sisters? How many older and how many younger?

20. What do you remember about the house you grew up in?

21. What is your I.Q.?

22. What religion do you practice if any?

23. What is your race or nationality?

24. What is your place in your community? (leader among friends, clubs, sports)

25. What are your political affiliations?

26. What do you do for amusement? (hobbies, books, newspapers, magazines you read, TV programs you watch if applicable)

27. What about the neighborhood you grew up in and what were some of the special occasions in your family? (holidays, reunions, picnics, vacations, etc.)

28. name some of the special homemade foods you ate as a child.

29. Name and describe some of the games you played as a child.

30. What is your favorite childhood memory?.

31. What is your worst childhood memory?

32. What was/is your relationship with your family. Describe in detail.

33. What year of school did you complete?

34. What is your sex life like and what are your morals?

35. What is your personal ambition and premise?

36. What are your chief frustrations and disappointments?

37. What subjects in school do you excel in?

38. What is your basic temperament? (choleric, easygoing, pessimistic, optimistic) 39. What is your general attitude toward life? (resigned, militant, defeatist, etc.)

40. Do you have any complexes? (obsessions, inhibitions, superstitions, manias, phobias) 41. During your schooling years what was your overall grade point average?

42. What did/do you like best about school?
43. Are you an extrovert, introvert? Describe.
44. What special abilities do you possess? (languages, talents)
45. What are your best and worst qualities? (imagination, judgement, taste, poise)
46. Are you now a member of any clubs, organizations, or religious congregations?
47. Did you ever smoke? (when, why and how much?)
48. What is your favorite drink, alcoholic and nonalcoholic?
49. What section of the newspaper do you read?
50. What do you enjoy doing most in your free time?
51. Do you read the newspaper?
52. What kind of music do you enjoy listening to?
53. What have your read recently? (book, magazine) 54. How do you feel about your age?
55. What do you do for exercise?
56. What is your best feature?
57. If you could change one thing about yourself, what would it be?
58. What is your favorite meal?
59. What are your favorite foods?
60. List three of your favorite films if applicable.
61. Who are your favorite movie stars? (if applicable)
62. In what other forms of entertainment/recreation do you enjoy and/or take part?
63. What is your favorite sport? Do you follow it professionally?
64. What time do you usually retire?
65. What is your favorite time of day? Why?
66. What is your favorite season? Why?
67. Which do you prefer, city or country living? Why?
68. Do you like intimate parties or large gatherings? Why?
69. What is your favorite color and why?
70. What is your greatest fear?
71. What is your favorite sleeping dream?
72. What is/was your worst nightmare?
73. Who is your closest friend?
74. How would you like to spend your next vacation?
75. What type of clothing do you most like to wear?
76. What are your favorite TV programs?
77. What would you enjoy doing on an evening out?
78. What would you like to be when you grow up? or What do you wish you had become?
79. What is your favorite animal? Why?
80. What are your prejudices?
81. Do you consider yourself an indoor or an outdoor person?
81. Do you consider yourself an indoor or an outdoor person?
82. What do you feel about war?
83. What do you feel about old age?
84. Do you have any old people in your life? If so, who?
85. Do you have any children in your life? If so, who?
86. Do you have medical insurance? If so, how do you feel about the coverage you get? If no, how do you feel about that?

87. Who was the last person you wrote a letter to and what did the letter say?
88. Are you happy with your lot?
89. Have you ever considered suicide?
90. What do you feel the future holds?
91. How do you feel about each of the other people you meet in this play/story?
92. Can you play a musical instrument?
93. Can you dance? If so, do you dance? If no, why not?
94. What did you do on your last birthday?
95. If you celebrate your birthday with others who was in attendance?
96. In school who was your favorite teacher? Why?
97. As a child how were you punished? (beaten, sent to room, time-out chiar, mouth washed out with soap)
98. As a child how were you praised or rewarded? (With money, food, gifts)
99. Where have you been moments before you make your first entrance in the play?
100. When you exit the play for the final time if you could have your way how would things turn out?

ASK QUESTIONS THROUGH YOUR CHARACTER
NOT HAVE LISTED ABOVE

1. _____
2. _____
3. _____
4. _____
5. _____
6. _____
7. _____
8. _____
9. _____
10. _____

TELLING THE STORY &
CREATING THE CHARACTER THROUGH COSTUMES

Every garment worn in a scene is considered part of the costume. Costumes are one of many tools the director or actor has to tell the story. Costumes communicate the details of a character's personality to the audience, and help actors transform into new and believable people on screen.

In real life, clothes define our taste and are an expression of our personality. It's rare that people wear new clothes each day. On a typical day, a teenager might wear a favorite well-worn skirt, a pair of earrings from the local mall, her mom's sweater and a birthday scarf from her best friend. When a movie begins, we meet the characters for the first time, and like us, each character is dressed in clothes that reflect their unique personality and style.

COSTUME, WHERE YOUR CHARACTER PURCHASED IT AND COST:

_____	_____	$ _____
_____	_____	$ _____
_____	_____	$ _____
_____	_____	$ _____
_____	_____	$ _____
_____	_____	$ _____
_____	_____	$ _____
_____	_____	$ _____
_____	_____	$ _____
_____	_____	$ _____
_____	_____	$ _____
_____	_____	$ _____
_____	_____	$ _____

PROPS: BUILDING YOUR CHARACTER THROUGH PROPS

Go through the entire script page by page, making notes on your spreadsheet of every item mentioned, as well as any inferred items. For example, a stage direction might say "the phone rings" and you would write down that there needs to be a phone in such-and-such scene.

Once you have created your initial script scan, sit down with the other actor(s) and go through the props list to see if any props have been added or omitted. From the example above of "the phone rings," the director may indicate that the actor actually goes offstage to answer the phone, so an actual phone prop is not actually necessary.

Scene Title:

_____

Actors: _____   _____   _____

Prop Item	Page	Actor	Location of Prop	Notes

ACTORS KNOWING YOUR CAMERA ANGLES

Whether creating your own content or acting in a major studio production, understanding the filmmakers' craft will improve your performance and make you the crew's best friend. Dipping your toe into film and television? Here are nine basic shot types that all on-camera actors should know!

The Establishing Shot
Remember the outside of Jerry Seinfeld's favorite diner or the house on the hill in "Psycho"? Frequently used in '90s sitcoms and classic films, the establishing shot is an extremely wide view—often an exterior—used to the indicate the place, time, or concept of the scene that follows. While it may not contain any actors, placement of characters within the establishing shot can be a great tool for indicating relationship before the start of the scene.

The Master Shot
The master differs from the establishing shot in that it covers all of the action of the scene, providing a wide view that will later be cut with tighter angles and close ups. Since it is often the first shot to be filmed, actors help the director out by choosing a physical action that can be repeated take after taking without hindering the creative process.

The Tracking Shot (or Dolly Shot)
This complicated shot follows the movement of actors, objects, or vehicles in the frame by mounting the camera on a dolly or using a skilled Steadicam operator. Frequently used in action movies and episodic television—think gurneys wheeling through an ER or swift walks through the White House hallway—tracking shots require focus, precision, and patience from crew and actors alike.

The Wide Shot (or Long Shot)
The wide shot gives the audience a sense of environment by showing an actor or actors from far away, generally framed from the top of their heads to the bottom of their feet. There is some room for movement within the frame, though wide shots are used sparingly and (usually) for only a small part of the scene.

The Two-Shot
The two-shot is just what it sounds like: two subjects together in a semi-tight frame. It can take several forms, from a mostly still shot used to establish the relationship between two characters to an action shot with two actors in frame.

The Over-the-Shoulder Shot
This popular method for shooting two characters tightly focuses on one actor while framing

the shot over the other actor's back and shoulder. This helps the audience focus on one speaker at a time while framing them in the context of their conversation. Since the second actor is only seen from behind, major film and television sets occasionally substitute a stand-in or photo double for over-the-shoulder shots.

The Medium Shot

Generally defined as a semi-close shot that shows actors from the hips up, this shot is used to capture subtle facial expressions while still depicting body language and environment that might be lost with a tighter frame.

The Close-Up

There's a reason Norma Desmond croons, "Alright Mr. DeMille, I'm ready for my close-up!" The close-up shot is arguably the actor's most important moment on set and requires a high level of focus and skillful subtlety. Close-ups are usually framed from the shoulders up and capture even the tiniest facial variations. Pro-tip: Actors can save their editors a major headache by avoiding overlapping dialogue in close-up scenes. It's easy to manually add overlap when cutting close-ups together, but near impossible to remove it; for this reason, most directors prefer "clean dialogue" with a small space between each line.

The Extreme Close-Up

The extreme close-up depicts intense emotion or fear by focusing very tightly on one small part of the actor's face, such as a roving eye or tightening lip. Artistic, dramatic, and bold, this shot is used sparingly but effectively in high-tension films and television shows!

SELF-TAPING FOR ACTORS – THE NEW NORM

Today's technology is allowing actors the convenience of self-taped auditions. More and more casting directors are having actors send in their own self-taped auditions to be seen for the part without having to come in and audition in person.

Occasionally, this may be in addition to a more traditional way of auditioning which helps to filter out a good chunk of candidates, and this saves time for both actors and casting directors. On top of saving time, there are other great benefits to self-taped auditions: actors don't have to travel, which saves money on gas, and of course it gives the actor much more control over their audition.

However, if you're an actor who is used to a more traditional way of auditioning in a casting room, you may find self-taping your audition a little daunting, especially due to lack of feedback. It does get easier and more comfortable the more you self-tape your auditions, and it won't be long before you'll be an expert at it, producing high quality auditions via self-tapes.

QUALITY OF YOUR SELF-TAPED AUDITION

The first thing you should remember with self-taped auditions is that the casting director and the team will not expect to see film quality that resembles a high budget Hollywood movie. CDs fully appreciate that you are doing it yourself with your own equipment, for instance a cheap video recorder, a DSLR camera or your mobile phone. Try and make your self-tape as professional as you can but don't worry about the tape appearing off center for instance.

THE IMPORTANCE OF LIGHTING

Obviously, the light where you are taking the self-tape audition won't be of professional quality, but it is somewhat important. Lighting can make or break your look and the casting director has to be able to see you clearly.

There are a few easy things you can do to ensure a good light for your self-tapes. Definitely choose a room that's well-lit and always make sure that there are no light sources behind you. Don't stand in front of a window when you are self-taping your audition, as being in front of a light will make you appear dark and the casting director will find it hard to see you.

Always do a test run first and then play it back. If you see that you are dark in the pictures, then find another area where the light may be better for filming. It is a matter of trial and error but it has to be spot on, otherwise you won't be seen properly and that could potentially get your self-tape "thrown into a bin" even if your acting is good.

CHOOSE YOUR BACKGROUND CAREFULLY

When recording a self-tape audition, the background is also very important. An ideal background is usually a blank one. Doors have always been a popular background, but if that's not an option for you than just try and find a background where not much is going on (no patterns, nothing to distract the Casting Director from you and your face) and with the least amount of things behind you.

The less distractions are in the background the better, and that will make your audition more pleasing to the casting director and the rest of the team watching you.

The easiest way you can do this if you're recording a self-tape at home is to grab a single-color blanket, or sheets, and throw them on the wall behind you. Pick colors that favor your face and make you stand out. Grey often works well. And, if you can spend a little extra, you can grab a green screen backdrop or something like that on Amazon; they're usually cheap.

CLOTHING CHOICE FOR SELF-TAPES

Choosing clothes for your self-tape audition can also be an important consideration, and you really want to be wearing a solid color. Clothing that's free from very bright and busy patterns works best for self-taped auditions. Keep your clothing as simple as you can and try to avoid too many accessories or jewelry.

Another thing that needs to be mentioned is that the camera does tend to add extra weight to your body. So ideally you don't want to be wearing clothes that aren't too tight or clothes that appear too big on you. Wear what you're comfortable with and just try and be yourself. Simplicity will work best here, unless you're aiming at specific character choice.

APPLYING MAKE UP

If you want to show off your features, then applying makeup will do this perfectly. The camera can make people looked a little washed out so makeup will work really well to prevent this. Apply your make-up many times and check how you look after each application to see what looks best for you when you're on camera. This may also boost your confidence. Just remember to keep your make-up to a minimal and do only the most essential things.

SHOW THEM WHAT YOU ARE MADE OF

If you already have auditioning instructions for your self-tape, then you know what you have to say or do specifically. If you do have instructions then just follow them, but if there are no specified instructions then just carry on how you would for a regular audition.

Remember to slate first. You should state your name, and then go on to say the name of the character you are auditioning for. Your slate should be friendly, and it should also show you are confident at your audition; do not be robotic. This is your first chance to show that you are a professional and that you have a personality. First impressions can be ruined by appearing too monotone, and a little personality goes a long way not only for self-taped auditions but in the acting business in general. It's vague to say, "don't be boring," but most of us usually know what that means.

STOP FILMING WHEN THE TIME IS RIGHT

This is easier said than done, but you have to know when enough is enough and when it's time to press that stop button for good. It is very easy to film one take and then watch it, then decide something isn't right and so you carry out another take and watch it and then decide something else is wrong.

Doing this over and over can end up driving you crazy and even though you definitely should try plenty of takes to get that best shot, remember that you do have to stop at some point.

The best advice here would be this: after you "warmed up" to your camera (1-2 takes), try doing a single take best shot just a couple of times and consider it done. Try and approach it the way you would traditionally as if you were auditioning in front of the casting director in person. Give the very best performance you can give on the first "real" take.

If you have to carry out more than one or two takes, allow yourself just one more and then stop, that's it; send your self-tape audition tot the casting director and move on.

FOLLOW THE SUBMISSION INSTRUCTIONS CORRECTLY

At this point, you've successfully completed your self-tape audition and you're happy with it. Now it's time to send it in. Make sure you follow instructions on how to send in your self-taped audition correctly and check over and over again that you have done all that needs doing.

Do you have to upload your audition onto a website? Or are you meant to send it via email? Are they asking for your resume and headshots alongside the self-tape? Are they asking for your clothing size or other measurements?

Always make sure you are providing the casting director with your correct email address and phone number for when they get back in touch with you. Try to keep this organized and professional.

FINAL THOUGHTS

As you can see, recording a self-tape audition can be an exciting process that gives you more control of your audition than you would get when auditioning in person. You get to record your audition in the comfort of your own home, with as many tries as you wish, and you send it in whenever you feel that it's ready to go.

Self-tapes are becoming very popular right now, and honestly, it's a great way to audition for parts outside of your area, or when you're lacking time. This is much more convenient than having to attend traditional auditions.

THE MAIN THINGS TO REMEMBER

- Always be yourself and show your personality
- Stay confident and focus on a single-take delivery
- Choose an area with good lighting or improve lighting yourself
- Make sure you can be heard and seen well
- **Have a good reader to read lines with you!**

Now it's time to apply for more projects, even if they're outside of your area, and start recording those self-tapes.

HOW TO STAND OUT AT THE AUDITION

As an actor, it may be hard to assess what the casting directors, producers and directors are looking for. Talent is definitely a huge part of what lands you a role, but personality and charisma are definitely included into the equation.

In addition to your talent, casting directors want to cast someone who stands out from the rest of the actors and leaves a lasting impression.

Here are some tips to help you stand out so that you can shine at your next audition

Be Prepared

Being prepared in every possible way is sure to make you stand out as a true professional. i.e.: Be warmed up, physically and vocally, have your headshot and résumé (plus extra copies), carry your sides, know the character, understand the project and the tone of the script, and be aware of who's in the room. As the saying goes, "Success happens when preparedness meets opportunity.

Be On time

Being on time is super important. Perhaps you won't stand out for being on time, but you'll definitely stand out for being late- and not in a good way. Being on time shows that you are a professional and you value both your time and the casting director's time.

Slate Professionally

Having proper audition technique is a must. Slate accordingly and don't do any 'green' actor ticks that make you look like a newbie or a hack. No last-minute tongue twisters in front of casting or strange turns into character. Say your name, take a beat, and begin.

Dress Appropriately

No matter what the character, dress in a way that shows a hint of them. If you're auditioning for a Queen don't wear a ballgown, but simply something that shows you have class and poise. Most importantly, always dress with respect for yourself.

Make a positive first impression

Come in prepared for your audition. Know what the project you are auditioning for is about. Have your research completed. If you are auditioning for an episodic show, watch the show and become familiar with the characters and story lines.

Make specific choices about your character

Prior to arriving for the audition, determine the specifics about the character. These specifics are up to you. When you are deciding about these choices, it is your time to use your creative imagination.

Be polite and positive to everyone

Not only should you respect the casting directors, but you should be courteous with the assistants or interns assisting with auditions. You are making an impression on how you treat people and what you would be like to work with for several days, weeks or months on a production. No one wants to work with someone who has a reputation for being unpleasant and believe me whenever someone's bad reputation precedes them, we always hear about it.

Proper Wardrobe Choices:

Make outfit choices that reflect what the character might wear. While you do not need to go over the top with a full-blown costume, getting the essence of the character will show the us that you familiarized yourself with the role. Suggesting a "hint" of the wardrobe also helps you get into character. For example, if you are playing a lawyer in a scene, then it is a good idea to come into the audition wearing a suit or looking professional.

Communicate:

When your come into audition, and a casting director or director asks a question, don't reply with one-word answers. We ask, "*How are you doing today?*" Actor says: "*Fine.*" Be a person and engage in conversation if the casting director, director, producer is willing to do so. Part of us asking questions and chatting a bit is how we see your personality.

Show How You Envision the Part

When auditioning, interpret the character the way you feel and see the role. Show your unique voice as you bring the script alive. Don't try to be what you think the casting director wants to see.

Don't Request or Expect Feedback

Everyone at the audition is there to work. Casting directors aren't there to coax you or direct you. They're looking for the actor they feel is right for the part. Be confident in yourself and your performance. If you're given direction, use it and respond professionally. But don't ask for feedback.

THE BRANDED ACTOR

As an actor, your personal brand is your "story." It's the image that you want casting directors, producers, and your fans to remember when they think of you. Just like a corporate brand; your personal brand explains who you are. It's what you stand for, which values you embrace, and how you express those values

What is an **actor's brand**? 'An idea made tangible by a human being (instead of a product)' Your **brand** should encompass who you truly are – not a 'cooler' version of you, but your authentic self. As an **actor**, the golden word is authenticity – not only in your work, but also in your life.

So, what's a personal brand?

"Your personal brand is the powerful, clear, positive idea that comes to mind whenever other people think of you. It's what you stand for — the values, abilities, and actions that others associate

with you. It's a professional alter ego designed for the purpose of influencing how others perceive you and turning that perception into opportunity."

So, you can see that personal branding is everywhere. We all have developed a personal brand over the years (most of us without even realizing it) that other people use to associate us with certain things. So, like the quote stipulated, personal branding is all about recognizing what your brand is and using its strengths to your advantage. As an actor, it's going to be essential that you realize your brand and make sure you cultivate it yourself, instead of letting it be the one to define you.

Actors often think they need to morph themselves and change their label every time they want to get work when the opposite is true. They need to choose who they are, plant their flag in the sand and say, "this is who I am" and keep saying it over-and-over again so people will want to buy it.

But actors tend to try to please every customer they meet by changing who they are and not understanding that getting hired starts with choosing a brand for themselves and sticking to it, regardless.

Make it Happen
Casting Directors see hundreds of headshots and audition videos a week, so you need to make your brand pop when they see your profile or videos.

It should be an identity that is easy to understand. For example, if you're a fitness brand, then take advantage of having an secondary headshot that shows off more of your physique, and create a mini reel, separate of your main reel, that has footage highlighting your athleticism or body type.

The easier it is for Casting Directors to understand who you are as an actor, the more you'll be considered for roles that actually match who you are, increasing your chances at being cast.

Casting Websites
Every actor should have updated profiles on casting websites like Actors Access. If you don't know about them, I've established a list of all the casting sites you should consider here. This is the perfect place to start branding yourself because you directly control what agents and Casting Directors see whenever you are submitted for an audition. Think of your actor profile like selecting a Netflix movie. Every time you stop on a movie, Netflix shows you a preview, and if you can't categorize it or see its best qualities then you're going skip to the next movie. Likewise, if the Casting Director is confused by your actor branding, they may skip over you.

Acting Training
This aspect an actor's career comes up time and time again because it is so very important. Through your training you will be honing what it is that you are actually marketing your talent and your skill. There is no cutting corners on this one! Discover what it is that you have a special talent for and be able to demonstrate it. Great comedic timing? Shakespeare? Stage Combat? You can

discover all this through taking class, and in doing so will pick up more strengths to add to your repertoire. Training is a key aspect and first step in marketing for actors.

Acting Cover Letter

You should have a strong acting cover letter that you can send potential agents, directors and producers this letter should be professional yet have something about it that makes you stand out from the rest so try and let your personality show through. Think of it as an introductory advertisement for yourself. This can be a hard thing to get right so keep working at it, try and find some inspiration in advertisements on TV, in magazines and in local trade papers.

Professional Resume

Another key element in marketing for actors is an uptodate actor resume. It should have on it all your relevant information and any training you have done as well as previous experience in theatre, TV and film. If you have a lot of experience just choose to list those roles that you think best sell your skill set. To see some examples of resumes and to find out more information on how to write them visit this page on the website.

Acting Reel

Much like your resume, you should get a professional to make your reel. They will edit it in a way that will make the most of what you have to offer, and that professional touch is worth every dollar. Your reel can have snippets of any film and TV roles that you have performed. Your reel should showcase your talent so try and get the scenes in that really show what you can do, and try and show some versatility. The same goes if you are trying to break into the voiceover market, you should get some help putting together a demo tape that is a recording of what you have to offer as a voiceover artist.

Actor Website

A more standard and nowadays traditional aspect of marketing for actors is having an actor website. This is becoming a very popular medium of late among aspiring performers, due to the fact that you can have a lot of information in one easy to view place. For a relatively small amount you can register your named domain site and use it as a place to have your resume, headshot and reel to be viewed by whoever visits your acting website.
Marketing For Actors: What else can you do?

Acting Career Promoting and Actor Marketing Activities

Successful self-promotion for actors is crucial to the success of an acting career. The problem is that so many actors are at a loss for how to get their work seen. I have found that many actors believe that all that is necessary to start an acting career is to "be able to act". Some don't even think that is necessary. The more a person who wants to become an actor knows about marketing and selling themselves, the more likely it is that they will be able to enjoy a sucessful acting career.

Social Media for Actors

Nowadays, almost everyone has a Facebook, Twitter, Vine and/or Instagram account; some with thousands, if not millions, of followers. Casting directors are not oblivious to this and in the past five years, casting calls and breakdowns are regularly being seen with 'actor must have good social media following / established social media name needed'. If you find social media a little difficult to follow or you've not considered using it, I urge you to start now!

Actor Branding (Building a Digital Brand)

Your personal brand is the powerful, clear, positive idea that comes to mind whenever other people think of you. It's what you stand for — the values, abilities, and actions that others associate with you. It's a professional alter ego designed for the purpose of influencing how others perceive you, and turning that perception into opportunity.

Acting Career Mentoring

A good acting career mentoring coach can help you put together a plan that will help you to market yourself in the right ways according to the type of actor you are. A really good coach should be well versed in marketing for actors.

ACTORS ON MAXIMIZING YOUR SOCIAL MEDIA EXPOSURE

The lack of an online presence through social media greatly hinders your ability to generate awareness for your brand and even get noticed by casting directors

The big three when it comes to an actor's social media presence are Twitter, Instagram, and Facebook, each of which can and should serve a different purpose. But there are others that can fulfill the particular needs of an actor in a number of ways, too; YouTube and LinkedIn among them.

Building an audience is important for any actor or filmmaker. Every acting job you do, each day on set or piece of content you create is an opportunity to build your audience. Here are 32 ways you can grow your following on social media.

NEW: Instagram now has over 1 billion users in 2021. That is the answer to the question, what will be the next big thing.

Social Media Apps You Should Know in 2021

Facebook   Twitter   LinkedIn   Instagram
Snapchat   TikTok   Pinterest   Reddit
YouTube   WhatsApp   Facebook Messenger
WeChat   Douyin   QQ   Sina Weibo   Telegram
QZone   Kuaishou Quora   VKontakte   Clubhouse

Handling Your Social Media Sites

1. Makeover your social media bios!
Your bio is a mini advertisement for why someone should like, subscribe or follow you! Tell us what you do, what you stand for and what you love! If you have a YouTube account, your 'About' section is your bio. This is where you can sell your channel to potential subscribers. Tell them how they'll benefit by watching your channel and why they should subscribe.

2. Optimize your profile photo.
If you're an actor this should be your headshot. Make sure you use this photo on all your social networks so you're recognizable to your fans.

3. Design your header, cover photos and YouTube Channel Art.
These are all a part of your crucial first impression and help visitors decide whether or not to follow you. This real estate should tell us about who you are and should include your social icons (to cross promote and build your audience on other platforms).

4. Create a Custom Snapcode.
If you are using Snapchat, customize your unique snapcode to match your website or the branding for your film. Be sure to add that Snapcode to your your site and social media.

5. Username Consistency.
Make it easy for your followers and fans to find you by using consistent usernames for yourself or your projects across all your platforms.

6. Find the people you already know!
Connect your email, other social networks, or your phone number (on Snapchat) to find the industry contacts you've already made.

7. Add follow buttons to your website.
Whether it's an actor website or a landing page for your film, always include social media icons and follow buttons to convert your visitors to followers. Want to go one step further? Add your twitter or Instagram feed or Facebook timeline to your site.

8. Add some tabs to your Facebook page.
Add an Instagram feed and Twitter tab to your Facebook page.

9. Use Hashtags on Facebook, Twitter and Instagram.
Knowing how to use hashtags correctly is fundamental to growing your audience on Twitter and Instagram. Hashtags allow your content to be discovered by new people who can follow you.

10. Add a watermark to your YouTube videos!
YouTube allows you to add a branding watermark to your videos (in your channel settings) that allows non-subscribers to become subscribers with one simple click.

11. Add your social usernames to your business card.
After making a connection with someone in person sometimes it's easier to ask to connect on social media than asking for a phone number or email.

12. Include your social icons & snapcode in your email signature.
Every email is an opportunity to build your audience!

13. Narrow your audience on YouTube.
Novice content creators create random videos that they think everyone will like. By trying desperately to appeal to everyone, you end up appealing to no one. Think hard about who you're creating content for. By being specific you will actually attract more of the right audience.

14. Try Live tweeting!
Are you on TV tonight or do you write or work on a show that's on TV tonight? Join the live conversation to connect with fans!

15. Take over an influencer's account!

If you're guest starring on TV or you're in an off-Broadway or Broadway show, see if you can do an Instagram or a Snapchat story takeover for an influential account to get access to their social media following.

16. Host a follower contest for your film!
The possibilities are endless here! The winner could win a day on set, a background role, or a special online screening and all it costs to enter is a like or a follow! You can even share your contest with influencers to reach a wider audience.

17. Create a trailer for your YouTube channel.
This trailer will autoplay for people who are not already subscribed to your channel. Keep your trailer short, exciting and end with a call to action to subscribe.

18. Join scheduled industry chats!
Participate in Twitter chats for actors or filmmakers or create your own chat to promote your content or theatre company.

19. Share other people's content.
Repeated sharing is caring, and many times is acknowledged by a retweet, a follow or a like. If sharing someone's image or article be sure to always tag or mention the creator of the post. They may retweet your post and you'll be introduced to their audience.

20. Clean up your Twitter account.
The more influential you appear the easier it is to get that 'follow' on Twitter. Are you following way more people than are following you? Flip this ratio by occasionally unfollowing people who have decided not to join your party on Twitter.

21. Get Verified on Twitter!
This goes with #20. Getting verified increases your credibility and will increase your follow back ratio. It's much easier to get verified as a personal brand than it used to be.

22. Ask to be "Suggested" on Snapchat.
Regularly ask your followers to 'suggest' your account to others (using the 'suggest' arrow on your profile), just like how you'd ask for a retweet, like, or subscribe.

23. Create eye-catching thumbnails on YouTube.

Your thumbnail is like a mini movie poster for your content. Its only job is to get people to watch! Bright, high-resolution, compelling thumbnails (containing the title) usually perform very well. Your video can come up in search, but if your thumbnail is boring no one will click on it (and, obviously, never subscribe).

24. Create a Snapchat geofilter for your show, film premiere or theatre company!

Snapchat has some simple guidelines to get you started. Encourage attendees to take photos at intermission, add your geofilter, and share them on social media using #YourShowsHashtag for special discounts! This spreads the word about your show and will build your audience on the platform.

25. Create YouTube playlists!

Playlists (like this one) are one of the most underutilized growth hacks on YouTube since they show up in search results just like videos do. If you are creating a web series playlists are also a great way to ensure your audience will watch them the way you intended.

26. Network with artists on Snapchat!

Add your name to snapchat directories for artists or use an app like Ghost Codes to meet other artists who may be interested in your projects and content.

27. Promote your account on your other networks.

If you have the extra characters in your Twitter bio add your usernames for Snapchat & Instagram. Creatively tell your audience they should join you on your other networks for exclusive content.

28. Just ask them to Subscribe!

Don't assume that if someone liked your video they're going to subscribe. Invite your viewers to subscribe at the end of your video so they can receive even more awesome videos like the one they just watched.

29. Showcase the behind-the-scenes of your film or #actorslife!

Choose one platform to be your exclusive behind-the-scenes network (this works great on Snapchat or using Instagram Stories). Promote this 'exclusive' content to your existing fans on Facebook and Followers on Twitter to get them to build your audience on Snapchat or Instagram.

30. Comment on Other Facebook Pages (as Your Page).

This is a Rockstar way to get more exposure for your Facebook Page with a target audience. Find Pages where your audience is already having conversations and join in (be sure to comment as your page not your profile).

31. Post Consistently and Strategically!

When your visibility increases, so do your followers. However, don't just tweet and post at random times. Find the prime time your followers are on to maximize your every post. If your goal is to grow the audience on your YouTube channel, create a schedule for your content. People like structure and will be more likely to subscribe if they know how often they'll be getting a new video.

32. Engagement is key!

Find like-minded people in the business to engage with everyday. Reply, Retweet, Regram and React! You can also actively 'follow' interesting like-minded people on Instagram and Twitter and if you've done #1-3 above, they might just follow you back.

AUDITION PREPERATION | EXERCISES & DRILLS

An acting audition can be nerve-wracking under any circumstances. Adding a camera to the mix can make it even more challenging. Prepare for a filmed audition as you would for any type of interview. After speaking your name into the camera, ignore it for the rest of the audition.

As an actor, it's important to exercise every day. It is just like another job where you have to keep improving your skills. And a great way to improve skills is by practicing every day as much as possible.

Most of the actors today all do is just focus on auditions and not bother about practicing their skills. You have to understand acting is just like any other art form, be it dancing or singing, where constant practice is a must.

Yes, practicing acting at home is a little hard because most of the exercises require a partner to practice. But even without partners, it is possible to practice acting and you can practice several aspects of acting.

For example, you can practice sense memory, voice, physicalizing, attitude, characterization, etc.

Before you begin to practice, make sure you have the right material and the Right tool. Most of the actors don't have the right tools to even practice properly.

Please take a look at my personal preparation tool using these printable worksheets you will be able to create a well-detailed character in a very short time. This has helped in infinite gigs, auditions and, it will help you too.

With the following Audition Drills randomly pick up the sheet and select anyone, one at a time. Force yourself to quickly get off book and know exactly where the camera is to slate your name. Then know exactly where your sightline/eyeline is.

Example: Be off book for a few short drills and repeat the following. Then go on to the other Audition Drills

(1). To the camera: Hello I'm (NAME), reading for the part of Melissa
To your sightline (Speak Below)

(EXERCISE 1)
MELISSA

When I was a child, I was always starved for affection. Sure my mom and dad tried to buy me off Barbie dolls, Darla Princess phones and Private Instutttt... Schools. But they never really loved me the way that I wanted.

(2). To the camera: Hello I'm (NAME), reading for the part of Dave
To your sightline (Speak Below)

(EXERCISE 2)
DAVE

The key is to never, ever let them get the upper hand. If she says, "I love you." Just nod. If she says, I don't see you enough. Blow her off for a week. If she tells you she wants you to buy her dinner, Buy her a combo meal from McDonalds.

Follow the same way with the following original audition drills written by John Pallotta. Start with Drill Number 1 and work your way up to the advanced drills

ORIGINAL AUDITION DRILLS
Written by John Pallotta
(LEVEL I)

DAVE
Mike, look, woman are they enemies
and you have to treat them accordingly.

LAWYER 1
And what the hell was that all
about out there, you have some explaining to do. Dismissed!

AGENT 1
How could someone get that close to him to plant an explosive and not get caught. Especially all the security detail on him.

PROSECUTOR
Well counsel, you have your job and we have ours. As long as there is an investigation in process, we have no intention in walking away.

BRODES
I hope your well paid, considering
how dangerous the work is.

HANSON
Sorry for the drill, Mr. Richards,
we'll need statements, credit card receipts, that stuff.

KAPLAN
It definitely does and the only thing I despise more than an agent with an ego is-an-agent-with-an-ego.

AGENT 1 (ON IIIS RADIO)
Delta "E" Bass, under attack, do you read? Central, come in!
(Repeat.)
Delta "E" Bass, under attack, do you read? Central, come in!

LOPEZ
No. Your orders have changed,
Mustafa is no longer your responsibility.

MALE/FEMEALE
Oh, she trusts you. She trusts you
just as much as she trusts anyone. Who better to betray her, then you.

AGENT
It'll keep you occupied while I
figure out what to wear at your execution.

BARNETT
Thank you sir, appreciate that.
Something tells me you didn't come all the over here to tell me that.

MALE/FEMALE
Its not enough you're trying to
hang me. I got rope under the bed, lets do it now. Save the tax payers some money.

DRUG ADDICT
Fuck you, Mother Fucker! I'm not saying "JACK" till my Mother Fucking lawyer gets here.

RICH KID
Now run along, Dick and don't let the door hit you in the ass - Dick!

FEMALE
Are you saying that you've never had a female friend that liked you, more then Its say, a friend?

JILL

After all these years you still think you can just pick me up in some dive bar?

SUSPECT

I'm clean... I'm clean man, what the fuck do you want. Take my wallet, its on my front pocket. Just take it and leave man.

INFORMANT

I don't make it a habit of discussing things like that with my clients.

HOOKER

That's 350 roses for a half hour, 600 roses for an hour, and Greek is on the menu for an additional fee.

OFFICER

I would have never had volunteered for this mission if I didn't think we had a chance coming home.

DATE

No. Look. When I kiss someone on a date, I like to exactly what I'm kissing.

DACKS

Fucking asshole, does the name Angela Grant ring a bell, Fran.

MALE/FEMALE

Mind of I stop and grab my
toothbrush before we head to your place.

ADVANCED AUDITION DRILLS
(LEVEL II)

MELISSA

When I was a child, I was always starved for affection. Sure, my mom and dad tried to buy me off Barbie dolls, Darla Princess phones and Private Instutttt... Schools. But they never really loved me the way that I wanted.

DAVE

The key is to never, ever let them get the upper hand. If she says, "I love you." Just nod. If she says, I don't see you enough. Blow her off for a week. If she tells you she wants you to buy her dinner, Buy her a combo meal from McDonalds.

LAWYERS

Not to offend you counsel, but though we were once married, once. In there I don't see you as an ex-wife, partner or otherwise. I'm a lawyer, paid by a client to perform a service in a court of law.

LAWYERS

This woman, my client, that you are trying your darnedest to indict, is a model citizen and a role model to our community. There is absolutely no reason why you should be holding her. Unless you release her, I am going to slap you with legal proceedings.

AYMES

Its not a small thing Dave, were talking hundreds and hundreds of federal and state data bases that need to be altered. What is the FBI going to do about that? I know what your doing, your putting everything on the line to harbor a wanted suspect.

LOPEZ

You've been after him now for over three years. Not to point a finger at anyone but, you haven't gotten the job done.

MALE/FEMALE

True career advancement requires risk. Consider my offer carefully, she will never let you advance in this organization. I win! If you want to get ahead in this place, you'll assist me.

KILLER

Oh, your back to see the butcher, Agent Kelly. Am I really that fascinating? Or did you come back in hopes of learning the secret recipe behind my homemade chicken soup.

DETECTIVE

This is about as easy as it gets for me. I can shut this folder and walk out that door, and by the time I get a latte, you're in the system. A slam dunk for the DA.

DOMINATRIX

There is no one scenario to describe what I desire. Actually, what I look forward to the most is being with a DOM who will take the pleasure in realizing his darkest dreams, desires, and fantasies with me.

DETECTIVE

Let me tell you something, this job isn't easy. We get the call, we got to go and talk down a guy with a gun, some crazy raving psyche mad mother fucker in some grocery store. Or we have to put up with some kind of drug addicted fuck, like yourself. But we still do it, because this is our job.

DOCTOR

Listen to me, I don't care that its an election year and don't give a damn about the media attention. All I care is about my patient, and at the moment all he really needs more treatment and less politics.

FEMALE DOCTOR

Its been my experience that men like that have a tremendous amount of difficulty separating emotional despair from what we woman call responsibility.

DR AYMES

...Maybe! Its not like your gonna pull a rabbit out of a hat. Even you friends at the institute couldn't find a cure and they had all the resources at hand.

FEMALE

The problem with you is you don't see true love when its staring you right in the face. Lemme give you an example. The woman in the grocery store this afternoon. The way she dribbled all over as you spoke to her.

JILL

You're going to have to explain that one to me. Because as far as I'm concerned, you've been a smooth operator just like everyone else. Is this the part where I'm supposed to melt because you've seen inside my soul.

PERSON 2

With all due respect, I didn't request this assignment. You can rest assure that as soon as this mission is over, I'll be as pleased to leave as you are to see me go.

KEEP NOTES

Whatever you used to film it, play it back so you can see how you are improving. Keep notes below on things you need to work on.

_____

_____

_____

_____

_____

_____

_____

_____

_____

_____

_____

_____

_____

_____

_____

_____

_____

_____

_____

_____

_____

_____

_____

_____

_____

_____

_____

_____

CLOSING
"Acting is A State of Mind with John Pallotta."

John Pallotta is a master on-camera acting teacher and one of the most sought-after acting coaches in the industry today. John has almost 40 years of experience as an actor, playwright, director, producer and acting coach and has trained under such masters as Lee Strasberg, Stella Adler, Bobbie Lewis, Uta Hagen, Austin Pendleton, Wynn Handman as well as many others. John Pallotta's belief is that "Acting is A State of Mind". Today, that belief has become an industry standard in John's books and in his teachings across the country.

John has accomplished thousands of coaching sessions and has ignited and reignited the careers of some of the talent you see on TV today: including Emmy award winner Anna Chlumsky, Emmy Winner Johnny Alonso and more.

John Pallotta has written 23 plays for the stage and his works have been produced, read, developed and workshopped at such venues as the Actors Studio in New York City, Steppenwolf Theatre in Chicago, The Labyrinth Theatre in NYC, Playwrights Horizons in NYC as well as many venues across the United States.

John's focus as a teacher of the craft is to help each and every one of his students finds their own voice as an actor. Acting is a process. It is a journey of discovery. It is a living breathing process that happens each and every day and does not happen overnight. Becoming an actor is learning a new way of thinking and about the way you look at life. Just as you make choices in life that determine your success or your failure. It goes the same for your choices you make as an actor.

VISIT
JOHN PALLOTTA ONLINE AT
www.actorstheater.com

THE END

Printed in Great Britain
by Amazon

35040186R00029